EDGAR ALLAN POE

Raintree is an imprint of Capstone Global Library Limited, a company incorporated in England and Wales having its registered office at 7 Pilgrim Street, London, EC4V 6LB -- Registered company number: 6695582

www.raintreepublishers.co.uk
myorders@raintreepublishers.co.uk

ISBN 978 1 406 26644 3
18 17 16 15 14 13
10 9 8 7 6 5 4 3 2 1

British Library Cataloguing in Publication Data
A full catalogue record for this book is available from the British Library.

Summary: There has been a murder. Two, in fact -- and detective Auguste Dupin is on the case. With no leads, no suspects, and no clues, the case seems impossible to solve. However, Dupin is no ordinary detective. In fact, his explanation of the crime seems rather extraordinary. But it still happened, even if it doesn't seem humanly possible...

Art Director: Bob Lentz
Graphic Designer: Hilary Wacholz
Edited by Diyan Leake
Production by Victoria Fitzgerald
Printed in China by Leo Paper Products Ltd

THE MURDERS IN THE RUE MORGUE

BY EDGAR ALLAN POE

RETOLD BY CARL BOWEN

ILLUSTRATED BY EMERSON DIMAYA

What songs the Syrens sang, or what name Achilles assumed when he hid himself among women, although puzzling questions are not beyond all conjecture.

– Sir Thomas Browne, *Urn Burial*

MENTAL ACUMEN, WHEN ONE HAS IT, IS A GREAT SOURCE OF PERSONAL AMUSEMENT.

AND LIKE ATHLETES WHO HAVE EXCELLENT PHYSICAL SKILLS, THE MAN WITH ACUMEN LOVES TO SHOW IT OFF.

BUT TRUE ACUMEN IS RARE. IT IS NOT MERELY INTELLIGENCE, EITHER. INTELLIGENCE IS THE MIND'S RAW POWER, JUST AS STRENGTH IS THE BODY'S RAW POWER.

READING IS THE INTELLIGENT MAN'S EXERCISE. IT MAKES HIM ABLE TO HOLD MORE FACTS.

ACUMEN IS INTELLIGENCE WITH ATTENTION TO DETAIL.

ATTENTION TO DETAIL IS THE MIND'S SENSE OF PERCEPTION.

CHESS EXERCISES ONE'S PERCEPTION. IF YOU FAIL TO PAY ATTENTION TO ALL THE PIECES, YOU CAN MISS A MOVE AND LOSE THE GAME.

BUT TRUE ACUMEN COMBINES ALL OF THESE QUALITIES.

PLAYING CARDS IS ONE OF THE BEST EXERCISES FOR A MIND'S ACUMEN.

ONE NEEDS INTELLIGENCE TO REMEMBER THE GAME'S RULES AND THE CARDS' VALUES.

AND ATTENTION TO DETAIL CAN REVEAL AN OPPONENT'S STATE OF MIND AND PREDICT HIS MOVES. THEN THE PLAYER CAN MAKE THE RIGHT MOVES AT THE RIGHT TIME.

AND I LEARNED ALL I KNOW ABOUT ACUMEN FROM A MAN NAMED AUGUSTE DUPIN...

ONLY AT NIGHT DID WE VENTURE OUTSIDE TO ROAM THE STREETS OF PARIS.

IT WAS ON ONE SUCH NIGHT THAT DUPIN FIRST DEMONSTRATED HIS AMAZING ACUMEN TO ME.

DUPIN, HOW DID YOU KNOW WHAT I WAS THINKING?!

IT WAS SIMPLE.

SIMPLE? WHAT DO YOU MEAN?

LET ME EXPLAIN.

THE NEXT DAY, DUPIN AND I WENT TO THE POLICE STATION TO VISIT LE BON.

I FELT GREAT SYMPATHY FOR THE MISERABLE MAN. JAIL WAS NO PLACE FOR ONE LIKE HIM.

UNLESS DUPIN WAS WRONG ABOUT HIM.

I BELIEVE YOU ARE INNOCENT, ADOLPHE. I THINK I CAN PROVE IT TO EVERYONE.

BUT FIRST YOU MUST TELL ME WHAT YOU KNOW.

THE PREFECT OF POLICE WASN'T GLAD TO SEE DUPIN.

OH. IT'S YOU AGAIN.

Préfect de Police

WHAT DO YOU WANT, THIS TIME, DUPIN?

I WANT TO EXAMINE THE CRIME SCENE IN THE RUE MORGUE AND TALK TO THE WITNESSES.

THERE'S NO NEED. THE CRIME IS SOLVED. AN ARREST HAS BEEN MADE.

I DON'T WANT YOU STIRRING THINGS UP.

WITH ALL DUE RESPECT, PREFECT, YOU'VE ARRESTED THE WRONG MAN. THE TRUE KILLER IS STILL OUT THERE.

WHAT IF HE KILLS AGAIN BECAUSE YOU WON'T LET ME INVESTIGATE THIS CRIME? WHAT IF--

FINE! YOU WIN!

IF YOU'RE RIGHT--AS USUAL --THEN PROVE IT. LIVES ARE AT STAKE HERE, DUPIN.

I'LL MAKE YOU A LIST OF WITNESSES AND SEND WORD TO THE MAN GUARDING THE SCENE.

THE FIRST THING DUPIN WANTED TO DO WAS INSPECT THE BODIES OF THE MURDERED WOMEN.

THE EXAMINER MET US THERE. IT WAS HE WHO HAD TOLD THE POLICE EXACTLY HOW THE WOMEN DIED.

HE SHOWED US THE MOTHER'S BODY FIRST. SHE HAD DIED FROM HAVING HER THROAT CUT.

SOME OF HER BONES WERE BROKEN, TOO.

INTERESTING...

NEXT, WE SAW THE DAUGHTER'S BODY. IT WAS COVERED IN BRUISES AND SCRAPES.

MOST OF THEM CAME FROM BEING STUFFED UP THE CHIMNEY, THEN PULLED OUT.

BUT SHE HAD NOT DIED IN THE CHIMNEY. SHE HAD BEEN STRANGLED TO DEATH FIRST.

DOCTOR DUMAS SHOWED US THE TERRIBLE BRUISES ON HER NECK THAT PROVED IT.

I COULDN'T BEAR THE SIGHT OF THOSE POOR WOMEN.

HOW I HOPED DUPIN COULD EXPOSE THE MONSTER WHO HAD DONE THIS!

ARE YOU SO SURE HE COMMITTED THESE MURDERS?

MAYBE IT WAS THE OTHER MAN WHO HELD THE RAZOR, BUT THEY WERE BOTH THERE.

THAT MAKES THEM BOTH GUILTY IF YOU ASK ME.

WHAT CAN YOU TELL ME ABOUT THE OTHER MAN YOU HEARD?

HE WAS RUSSIAN.

NO, WAIT... SPANISH, MAYBE?

DO YOU SPEAK SPANISH? OR RUSSIAN, MONSIEUR MONTANI?

NO.

BUT THE FIRST MAN SPOKE FRENCH. I'M ABSOLUTELY CERTAIN.

BUT ARE YOU ABSOLUTELY CERTAIN IT WAS ADOLPHE LE BON'S VOICE?

I...
I GUESS NOT.

EXCEPT FOR THE CONFUSION ABOUT THE VOICES, ALL THE WITNESSES' STORIES WERE THE SAME...

NOW IT WAS TIME FOR US TO SEE THE CRIME SCENE FOR OURSELVES...

AN ORANGUTAN?!

YOU CAN'T BE SERIOUS, DUPIN...

CONSIDER THE SECOND VOICE THE WITNESSES HEARD THAT NIGHT.

IT BELONGED TO THE BEAST.

THAT'S WHY IT SOUNDED STRANGE AND FOREIGN TO ALL OF THEM.

AND WHAT ABOUT THE FIRST VOICE? THE ONE EVERYONE AGREED WAS SPEAKING FRENCH?

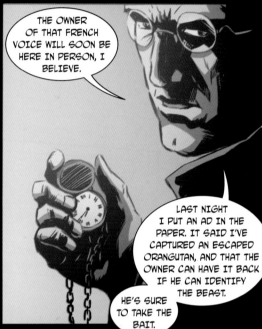

THE OWNER OF THAT FRENCH VOICE WILL SOON BE HERE IN PERSON, I BELIEVE.

LAST NIGHT I PUT AN AD IN THE PAPER. IT SAID I'VE CAPTURED AN ESCAPED ORANGUTAN, AND THAT THE OWNER CAN HAVE IT BACK IF HE CAN IDENTIFY THE BEAST.

HE'S SURE TO TAKE THE BAIT.

KNOCK

KNOCK

THE VISITOR WAS A SAILOR -- A FRIGHTENING-LOOKING ONE.

MONSIEUR, YOUR AD SAYS YOU FOUND MY ESCAPED PET?

I'M VERY HAPPY TO PAY YOU BOTH A REWARD. ANYTHING YOU WANT, REALLY.

THAT SOUNDS FAIR. LET ME THINK -- WHAT DO I WANT?

OH, I KNOW...

...YOU SHALL TELL ME EVERYTHING YOU KNOW ABOUT THE MURDERS IN THE RUE MORGUE!

WAIT! PLEASE DON'T SHOOT!

FRIGHTENED, RAZOR IN HAND, THE ANIMAL NOTICED THE L'ESPANAYE APARTMENT.

LIGHT GLOWED ON THE FOURTH FLOOR DESPITE THE LATENESS OF THE HOUR.

THE BEAST RACED TO THE WALL AND SCALED THE LIGHTNING ROD. THE SAILOR FOLLOWED.

BUT BEFORE THE SAILOR COULD REACH THE TOP, THE BEAST SWUNG ITSELF INSIDE USING THE SHUTTER.

WHEN THE SHUTTER SWUNG BACK, THE SAILOR CLIMBED ON TO IT. YET HE LACKED THE APE'S AGILITY.

ALL HE COULD DO WAS HANG THERE HELPLESSLY...

...AND WATCH.

MADEMOISELLE L'ESPANAYE FAINTED AT THE SIGHT OF THEIR SURPRISE GUEST.

THE APE THEN CREPT UP ON MADAME L'ESPANAYE.

DROPPING THE RAZOR, IT TURNED ITS ATTENTION TO MADEMOISELLE L'ESPANAYE.

IT SQUEEZED ITS LONG FINGERS AROUND HER NECK UNTIL SHE DIED.

ONLY THEN DID THE MADDENED BEAST NOTICE THE FACE OF ITS MASTER WATCHING.

Over the course of his life, Edgar Allan Poe submitted many stories and poems to a number of publications. Either they were rejected, or he received little or no compensation for them. His most popular work, "The Raven", quite nearly made him a household name -- but only earned him nine dollars.

Poe was unable to hold a single job for very long, jumping from position to position for most of his life. He had very few friends, was in constant financial trouble, and struggled with alcoholism throughout his adult years. Edgar's family rarely helped him during these difficult times. In fact, when Edgar's father died in 1834, he did not even mention Edgar in his will.

Though largely unappreciated in his own lifetime, Edgar Allan Poe is now recognized as one of the most important writers of literature in English.

THE RETELLING AUTHOR

CARL BOWEN is a father, husband, and writer living in Lawrenceville, Georgia, USA. He was born in Louisiana, lived briefly in England, and was raised in Georgia where he went to school. He has published a handful of novels, short stories, and comics. He has retold novels, stories, and plays, including *20,000 Leagues Under the Sea*, *The Strange Case of Dr Jekyll and Mr Hyde*, *The Jungle Book*, "Aladdin and the Magic Lamp", *Julius Caesar*, and this comic book. He is the original author of *BMX Breakthrough* as well as the Shadow Squadron series -- which includes *Sea Demon*, *Black Anchor*, *Eagle Down*, and *Sniper Shield*.

THE ILLUSTRATOR

EMERSON DIMAYA makes banner ads and websites by day, and illustrates comics by night. His tools of the trade include pencils, pens, and computer applications such as Photoshop, Illustrator, and Corel Draw. His dark, moody, and atmospheric style of illustration is inspired by his fascination with zombies, monsters, and other supernatural creatures. He is currently living with his wife and a dog on an island somewhere in the Philippines.

GLOSSARY

ACUMEN keen insight or intellect

AGILITY ability to move quickly and easily

ASTONISHING surprising and impressive

BIZARRE very strange or odd

CONTRARY opposite

CREPT moved slowly and silently

EXTRAORDINARY very unusual or remarkable

FRANCS main unit of money in Switzerland, many African countries, and formerly in France

LINGER stay or wait around

MORGUE place in which bodies are kept, especially the bodies of victims of violence, crimes, or accidents

PREFECT person appointed to any of several command positions, like the chief administrative official of a department in France

RECOGNIZE see or hear someone and know who that person is

SECLUDED quiet and private

SHRILL having a high, sharp, or harsh sound

SYMPATHY the understanding and sharing of other people's troubles

VISUAL QUESTIONS

1 What do the lines next to the orangutan's face mean? What is he thinking? (If you're not sure, check page 57 for clues.)

2. Why do you think the window, the body outline, and Dupin's glasses are red in this spread? What do you think is the purpose of the red colour accent throughout the book?

3. Based on what you know from the story, whose voice is saying "Sacre Diable!" in this panel?

4. Why are the orangutan's eyes red in the left panel, and white in the right panel? Why do you think the creators chose to do this? Check pages 52–57 for hints.

5. Dupin is a very intelligent man. Identify several panels in this book where he shows his impressive attention to detail, keen intelligence, or amazing acumen.

THE FALL OF THE
HOUSE OF USHER

WHILE MY COMPANIONSHIP DID SEEM TO HELP HIM A LITTLE...

...RODERICK'S SICKNESS WAS PROVING TO BE...

...INFECTIOUS.

Read all four

EDGAR ALLAN POE

graphic novels...

EDGAR ALLAN POE

THE
TELL-TALE
HEART

HARPER • CALERO

EDGAR ALLAN POE

THE FALL OF THE
HOUSE OF USHER

MANNING - JIMENZ

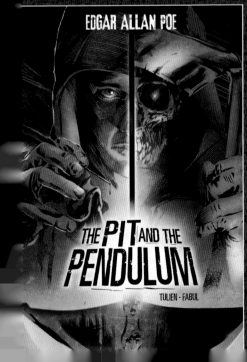

EDGAR ALLAN POE

THE PIT AND THE
PENDULUM

TULIEN - FABUL

EDGAR ALLAN POE

THE
MURDERS IN
THE RUE MORGUE

BOWEN - DIMAYA